Donated ~ 1979

# HE SETS
# THE
# CAPTIVE FREE

BY CORRIE TEN BOOM WITH JAMIE BUCKINGHAM
  *Tramp for the Lord*

BY CORRIE TEN BOOM WITH C. C. CARLSON
  *In My Father's House*

BY CORRIE TEN BOOM WITH
  JOHN AND ELIZABETH SHERRILL
  *The Hiding Place*

BY CORRIE TEN BOOM
  *Corrie's Christmas Memories*
  *Corrie ten Boom's Prison Letters*
  *He Cares, He Comforts*—JESUS IS VICTOR
  *Each New Day*
  *A Tramp Finds a Home*—NEW LIFE VENTURES
  *He Sets the Captive Free*—JESUS IS VICTOR

## Jesus Is Victor

# He Sets
# the
# Captive Free

## CORRIE TEN BOOM

Fleming H. Revell Company
Old Tappan, New Jersey

Scripture quotations not otherwise identified are based on the King James Version of the Bible.

Scripture quotations identified LB are from The Living Bible, Copyright © 1971 by Tyndale House Publishers, Wheaton, Illinois 60187. All rights reserved.

Scripture quotations identified PHILLIPS are from LETTERS TO YOUNG CHURCHES by J. B. Phillips. Copyright © 1947, 1957 by Macmillan Publishing Co., Inc., renewed 1975 by J. B. Phillips. Copyright © 1968 by J. B. Phillips. Used by permission.

Scripture quotations identified RSV are from the Revised Standard Version of the Bible, copyrighted 1946, 1952, © 1971 and 1973.

ISBN 0-8007-0929-2

*Copyright © 1977 Corrie ten Boom*
*Published by Fleming H. Revell Company*
*All rights reserved*
*Library of Congress Catalog Card Number 77-99134*
*Printed in the United States of America*

# Contents

# Preface

I know how it feels to be behind a door that can be opened only from the outside, for I have been a prisoner in three different prisons. I learned a great deal in prison, as this was a very difficult class in the schoolroom of life. When you are in a difficult class with a good teacher, you learn much—and my teacher was very good. It was Jesus Himself!

I wish I could share with you what I learned during my imprisonment, but I am old and I cannot travel much now. Since we cannot speak personally together, I have decided to visit you through this little book. The conversations, the experiences really happened to me and I want to share them with you—to show you that even when circumstances look utterly bleak, there is a victorious life which is real and available to you. ous life which is real and available to you.

It is not only behind barbed wire or prison doors that there are prisoners. There are prison-

ers of sin, of lust, prisoners of wrong philoso-
phies, prisoners of circumstances, prisoners of *self*. There are prisoners everywhere. I pray
that this book will help you too to lose your life
for Jesus' sake so that you may gain it. Jesus said
that those whom He makes free are free indeed.
Whether decent or indecent sinners, we all need
Jesus. He loves us. Yes, He loves you!

# HE SETS
# THE
# CAPTIVE FREE

# 1

# I Was in Prison

"Name?" the Interrogator inquired.

"Cornelia ten Boom, and . . . ."

"Age?"

"Fifty-two."

It was a dark night when we were finally marched out of the building. We could see before us a large canvas-roofed army truck. The truck had no springs and we bounced roughly over the bomb-pitted streets of The Hague. Leaving the downtown section, we seemed to be headed west, toward the suburbs of Scheveningen. Now we knew our destination; the Federal Penitentiary named after this seaside town of Scheveningen.

We turned left into an endless world of steel and concrete.

"Ten Boom, Cornelia!"

Another door rasped open. The cell was deep and narrow, scarcely wider than the door. A woman lay on the single cot, three others on straw ticks on the floor. "Give this one the cot," the matron said. "She's sick." . . .

Soon I was moved to another location. The cell was identical to the one I had just left: six steps long, two wide, a single cot at the back. But this cell was empty. As the guard's footsteps died away down the corridor, I leaned against the cold metal of the door. Alone. Alone behind these walls . . . solitary!

Weeks later, "Get your things together! Get ready to evacuate!" The shouts of the guards echoed up and down the long corridor. I was thankful to see other faces again, . . . but!

Where would we be taken? Where were we headed? One thing I dreaded . . . please . . . not into Germany!

Hours passed as the loaded train sat on the siding. It must have been two or three in the morning when the train at last began to move. The thought uppermost in every mind was : Is it Germany?

Finally we seemed to stop in the middle of a wood. Floodlights mounted in trees lit a broad rough-cleared path lined by soldiers with leveled guns.

Spurred on by the shouts of the guards, I started up the path between the gun barrels. "Close ranks! Keep up! Five abreast!"

The nightmare march lasted a mile or more, when at last we came to a barbed-wire fence surrounding a row of wooden barracks. We went into one of them and fell into an exhausted sleep. So began our stay in this place that we learned was named Vught, after the nearest small village. Vught had been constructed in Holland by the occupation army primarily as a concentration camp for political prisoners.

Several months later we were moved to another camp. After a night punctuated with the hail of bullets and machine-gun fire, we learned at dawn that we were passing through a border town into Germany. For two more incredible days and nights we were carried deeper and deeper into the land of our fears.

From the crest of the hill, we saw a vast scar on the green German landscape; a city of low gray barracks, surrounded by concrete walls on which guard towers rose at intervals. In the very center a square smokestack emitted a thin gray vapor into the blue sky.

"Ravensbruck!"

Like a whispered curse, the word passed back through the lines. This was the notorious extermination camp for women, whose name we had heard even in Holland.

Adapted from *The Hiding Place*

# 2

# Why I Was Sent to Prison

I want to tell you about my experiences in three prisons. During World War II, I was a prisoner of the Gestapo because my family, my friends, and I had saved the lives of Jewish people in Holland. Adolf Hitler was preparing to kill all of them, and our task was to help them to escape to safer countries.

When that was no longer possible, we hid them in our houses. In the end we had a group of eighty people with whom we worked to supply the desperate needs of a hidden people: food, clothing, houses, burials. There were many other factors facing a group of helpless persons hiding in a country already stripped by the occupying army of a powerful enemy.

We were betrayed and all were arrested. My father was eighty-four years old, and lived only a

short while in the prison where all his children
and a grandson were also incarcerated. We never
saw him again, for the prison walls separated us.

Father was a courageous man, but he understood that he was too old for prison life. "If I am
imprisoned, I shall die, but it will be an honor for
me to give my life for God's chosen people, the
Jews," he said before they arrested him. I heard
much later that he had died after only ten days'
imprisonment.

# 3

# Solitary Confinement

For the first week, they put me in a cell with four or five others, for I was very ill with pleurisy. The prison doctor said it would develop into tuberculosis, so I was sent to solitary confinement. He didn't want me to infect the others.

For the first time ever, I was really alone, and I knew my life was completely in the hands of the enemy. They could kill me or torture me or just forget about me altogether, and there would be no one to know or care.

At night the sounds of distant bombing penetrated the thick walls—and from somewhere within came the muffled cries of people being tortured by the Gestapo—that was a little bit of hell! When I lost courage, I tried singing, but the guards pounded on the door and demanded silence. They threatened to take me to the *dark* cell. In the dark cell you had to stand in water. Time became a very thick thing that I struggled to wade through.

Solitary confinement lasted four months. It wasn't only the isolation that was so hard, but the constant threat that at any moment of the day or night they would come for me. Whenever I heard footsteps outside my cell I would ask myself, "Are they coming to torture or kill me?"

Once I stood with my back against the wall with my hands spread out, as if to try to push away the walls that were closing in on me. I was dead scared. I cried out, "Lord, I'm not strong enough to endure this. I don't have the faith!"

Suddenly I noticed an ant which I had watched roaming the floor of the cell for days. I had just mopped the floor with a wet rag, and the moment the ant felt the water on the stones, he ran straight to his tiny hole in the wall.

Then it was as if the Lord said to me, "What about that ant? He didn't stop to look at the wet rag or his weak feet—he went straight to his hiding place. Corrie, don't look at your faith; it is weak, like the tiny feet of that ant. Don't dwell on the treatment you might receive from these cruel people. I am your hiding place, and you can come running to Me just like that ant disappeared into that hole in the wall."

That brought real peace into my heart. I was then fifty-three years old, and I had always known about Jesus, but there in solitary confinement I began to really understand and experience for myself that His light is stronger than the deepest darkness.

I know there are moments for you when you lose all courage. You feel as a prisoner that you don't exist in the eyes of the people around you, in the eyes of God, or in your own eyes. Then you can read in the Bible a promise from Jesus: "Come to Me, all you who have heavy burdens, and I will give you rest" (Matthew 11:28). When you can believe that, you will *know* Someone is still interested in you. Someone still cares about you—not as a number, but as a person.

# 4

# The Interrogation

After two months in the cell, I was called in for interrogation. The judges, the *Sachbearbeiters*, had a tremendous amount of power, and you had no rights whatever. They could give you a short sentence, a long sentence, or sentence you to death. You were totally in their hands.

I will never forget the moment when I was brought before my judge. I knew that not only my own life was in his hands, but that I could incriminate many friends and co-workers. If I were forced to tell about them, it could mean their death sentence, too.

I prayed for wisdom to answer all the questions of the interrogator, and there were *many* questions! I had to give my whole life history, even what I did in my spare time.

I told him that I taught a Bible class for fee-

bleminded people who could not go to church
because they could not understand sermons.
"They need the Lord Jesus just as much as you
and I do," I said to this National Socialist judge.

He replied, "What a waste of time! Isn't there
far more value in converting a normal person than
an abnormal one?"

My answer was, "If you knew Jesus, you would
know that He has a great love for everyone who is
despised or in need. It is possible that a poor,
feebleminded child has more value in His eyes
than you and I together."

He was angry when I said that, and he called
the policemen, saying, "Take her back to her
cell."

The next day I was brought again before my
judge, who said, "I could not sleep during the
night. I was thinking over what you had said
about Jesus. I don't know anything about Him.
We have plenty of time for the interrogation.
First, tell me what you know about Jesus."

Boy, was that an opportunity! I began, "Jesus is
a light come into this world. No one who believes
in Him remains in darkness. Is there darkness in
your life?"

His answer was, "Darkness? There is no light

at all in my life. I hate my work. My wife is in Bremen, Germany. I don't even know if she is still alive. The town is being bombed heavily every night now. It is possible that she was killed this very night."

Suddenly the contact between us was on a totally different level. He was no longer the judge, but simply a man in great need, and I, his prisoner, could give him real encouragement as I brought him the Gospel.

I said to him, "Jesus once said, 'Come to me, all who are heavy laden, and I will give you rest.' Come to me—*all*. That means you, too. Come unto Jesus and He will give you rest. Tell Him your sins. He has never sent away any sinner."

I had a good talk with that man, and from then on he was no longer my enemy, but my friend. He helped to save my life and did his utmost, though unsuccessfully, to set me free.

Of course, he still had to do his job, and so he showed me papers found in my house. To my horror I saw names, addresses, and particulars which could mean not only *my* death sentence but the death of my family and my friends as well.

"Can you explain these papers?" he asked.

"No, I cannot." I felt miserable. (You will say,

"Why did you have such dangerous papers in your house?" In our underground efforts to save Jewish people, I worked with many young people who did remarkably courageous work. But they were not always careful, so these papers were found in my house.)

The judge knew even better than I how dangerous those papers were. Suddenly he turned around, opened the door of the stove, and threw all the papers into the stove. At that moment it was as if I understood for the first time the text in Colossians 2:13, 14 PHILLIPS:

> . . . God has now made [you] to share in the very life of Christ! He has forgiven you all your sins: Christ has utterly wiped out the damning evidence of broken laws and commandments which always hung over our heads, and has completely annulled it by nailing it over His own Head on the Cross.

In heaven there are dangerous papers for us all, and whether we believe it or not, we will have to come before the judgment seat of God. If we have refused Jesus Christ in this life, then the Judgment Day will be terrible. But if we have received Jesus as our Saviour and Lord, then we have nothing to fear, because Jesus nailed these terrible papers to the Cross when He died for the sins of the whole world—your sins and mine. That is what I understood when I saw those papers destroyed by the flames in that stove.

Years later I met that judge in Germany, and I asked him, "Did you ever receive the Lord Jesus as your Saviour? Did you bring your sins to Him? It says in the Bible, 'If you confess your sins, He is faithful and just to forgive you, and He will cleanse you from all unrighteousness.' "

His answer was, "No, I did not do that. I am a very good man, and I have never committed sins."

"I am sorry you think that, because that means you cannot have salvation. Jesus will never ever send away anybody who comes to Him. But there is one kind of person in the Bible that I must tell you about.

"That was the Pharisee who said, 'I am good.' And Jesus could not and would not help him. If the time comes when you know you have sins, that you are a sinner, don't forget what I told you. The Bible tells us that Jesus has accepted our punishment at the Cross, and the only thing we have to do is to receive Him as our Saviour and come to Him and confess our sins."

He thought a moment and then suddenly said, "I know a sin that I have done."

I said, "All right—bring it to the Lord at once. Ask His forgiveness and thank Him for His forgiveness." He did.

Later in the evening he said, "I see another sin in my life."

"So, you know that you are a sinner. That is good. Just bring it to the Lord and ask forgiveness," I replied. When for the *fourth* time he remembered a sin which needed to be brought to the Lord, I knew he was ready to receive the Lord Jesus Christ as his Saviour.

I said, "Now you can accept Jesus. You know that you need Him."

He did, and I know that his sins were forgiven and that his name was written in the Book of Life.

# 5

# Ravensbruck

The Nazis were emptying jails everywhere! Male prisoners were sent in one division, and women prisoners in another. My sister Betsie and I, herded together with thousands of other women, were marched into Ravensbruck. It was called a work camp.

When we first came into this concentration camp, they took all our possessions. It was a real miracle that I was able to keep my Bible.

At great risk, I hid it on my back under my dress, and I prayed, "Lord, will You send Your angels to surround me?" Then I thought, *But angels are spirits, and you can see through spirits. I don't want these people to see me!* So I prayed then, in great fear, "Let Your angels *not* be transparent. Let them cover me."

And God did it! As we passed through the inspection, the woman in front of me was searched, then my sister, directly behind me, was searched—but I walked through unsearched!

Our barracks was built for four hundred women, but they packed fourteen hundred of us inside. Bunks were stacked all the way to the ceiling, and we each had a sleeping space only a few inches wide. When they were all working, we had eight toilets for the entire barracks!

In Ravensbruck it was dangerous to use the Word of God. If you were caught teaching the Bible, you were killed in a cruel way, but the guards never knew that I had a Bible meeting twice each day in Barracks 28. The one jammed room was filthy, crawling with fleas and lice, and the guards never came inside the door. You see how the Lord used both angels and lice to keep my Bible in our possession?

# 6

# Does He Forget Me?

Sometimes I experienced moments of great despair. I remember one night when I was outside the barracks on my way to roll call. The stars were beautiful. I remember saying, "Lord, You guide all those stars. You have not forgotten them, but You have forgotten Betsie and me."

Then Betsie said, "No, He has not forgotten us. I know that from the Bible. The Lord Jesus said, 'I am with you always, until the end of the world,' and Corrie, He is here with us. We must believe that. It is not what we are *feeling* that counts, but what we *believe!*"

> Feelings come and feelings go
> And feelings are deceiving.
> My warrant is the Word of God,
> None else is worth believing.

I slowly learned not to trust in myself or my faith or my feelings, but to trust in Him. Feelings come and go—they are deceitful. In all that hell around us, the promises from the Bible kept us sane.

Ravensbruck certainly *was* a work camp. It was the enemy's plan to work us—to death! Before the war ended, ninety-six thousand women died there. Even my dear Betsie became an old woman before my eyes and slowly starved to death.

The smoke from the crematorium was like a black haze over the camp. Every day seven hundred women died or were killed. There were far too many of us, and death was the only solution to the problem. I looked death in the eye day after day, and I found the Lord to be my refuge still, my only hiding place.

# 7

# The Lifeline

The greatest moment of your life can be when everything seems finished for you. That is the moment when you lay your weak hand in the strong hand of Jesus. For Jesus can make life and death—present and future—victorious! He can give you eternal life; not only life in heaven, but life right now.

It is as when you have fallen in the sea and you think: *Now I will surely drown. I can swim perhaps an hour, but then I will sink!* A lifeline is the only thing that can help you then.

I found that when you are drowning in the terrific misery of the world, Jesus is everything for you—your only lifeline. When you think you have lost everything, then you can be *found* by Jesus Christ.

He died for you. He lives for you, and He loves

you more than any human being can love. I have
told people about Him for thirty-three years, in
sixty-four countries, and in all that time nobody
has ever told me he was sorry he asked Jesus to
come into his life. You won't be sorry, either.

# 8

# A Storm Laid Down

Punishments were often general in Ravens-bruck. Once we suddenly heard shouting, beating, and swearing in our room. We lived in a crowded room, packed together. Everything was filthy and broken-down. Two people were sharing a very small bunk, and one had thrown the other out of the cot, so they started to fight.

Betsie said, "Corrie, we need to pray. This is dangerous!"

It *was* dangerous. If the guards had heard the fighting in our barracks, we would all have been cruelly punished. Betsie remained praying. She prayed and prayed. It was as if a storm died down. We heard less beating, less swearing and shouting. Finally, it was quiet, and Betsie said, "Thank You, Father. *Amen*."

Now, do you see what happened there? There

was a room with many prisoners in great danger, and there was one starving old woman—Betsie. God used Betsie to save the situation. That is what God is willing to do and is going to do with you and me when we let Him show us what to do—when He guides us.

The Bible says that we are representatives of heaven on this earth; that we are ambassadors for Jesus Christ. It is terribly important for the world that there are ambassadors—representatives from heaven—in this world, and you and I can be those ambassadors. Often it will save the situation and bless our surroundings. Because we do it so well? No, not at all. Because the Lord is using us to do what *He* wants done.

# 9

# No Wilderness, the Lord's Garden

"You must tickle the hand of God before He is willing to help you," said a prisoner who was sitting on the bed behind me.

"No, girl, that is not true. When you really know the Lord, you know that He is far more ready to bless us than we are ready to ask for His blessing. He loves us. The Bible says, 'You are God's field' " (*see* 1 Corinthians 3:9 RSV). The great preacher and writer C. H. Spurgeon expresses this very clearly:

Oh, to have one's soul as a field under heavenly cultivation,
No wilderness, but a garden of the Lord, walled around by grace,
Planted by instruction, visited by love,

34

Weeded by heavenly discipline, guarded by
  divine power.
One's soul thus favored is prepared to yield
  fruit unto the glory of God.

A garden does not do much. It does bring forth
fruit and flowers. But the one who has the respon-
sibility is the gardener, and it is He, our Gardener, who blesses us, surrounds us with grace,
and disciplines us. Whether we are willing or not,
He does the job. On our part it is necessary to
surrender, and then He makes His garden from
the wilderness of our lives. It is wonderful what
He is willing and able to do.

# 10

# Is Forgiveness Possible?

Do you know how it feels when your heart is full of hatred? We were working in an area where wrecked airplanes were piled together. We had to gather the many pieces and load them onto big trucks. It was terribly heavy work for us.

My sister Betsie was a very frail woman, and she could not lift much, but she did her utmost. Suddenly one of the guards noticed that Betsie was picking up only the little pieces, because the big pieces were too heavy for her.

Betsie said kindly to her, "Don't give me more to do than I am trying to do already, because I am not strong enough to lift these heavy parts."

The woman guard said, "You don't decide what you do. *I* decide." Suddenly the guard started to brutally beat Betsie. I have never been so enraged! The other prisoners held me back so I could not grab the guard.

When she had gone, I ran to Betsie, who had blood all over her face. She said, "No, don't hate, Corrie. You must love and forgive."

"I cannot! I am not able."

If there is hate in your heart, you cannot forgive. I knew this, and I also knew what Jesus had said:

> But if you do not forgive, neither will your Father who is in heaven forgive your trespasses.
>
> Mark 11:26

After we were back in our barracks, I climbed out of the window and went for a little walk alone, and I talked with the Lord. I said, "Lord, I cannot forgive that brutal woman. It is more difficult to forgive when people you love suffer than when you suffer yourself."

Then the Lord reminded me of a text. I had my little Bible hidden under my dress. I opened it and read:

> . . . God's love has been poured into our hearts through the Holy Spirit which has been given to us.
>
> Romans 5:5 RSV

Suddenly I saw that what *I* was not able to do, the Lord, in me, was able to do. I said, "Oh, Lord, I thank You for Romans 5:5. I thank You, Jesus, that You brought into my heart God's love through the Holy Spirit. Thank You, Father, that Your love in me is stronger than my hatred."

At that moment, when I was able to forgive, my hatred disappeared. What a liberation! Forgiveness is the key which unlocks the door of resentment and the handcuffs of hatred. It is a power that breaks the chains of bitterness and the shackles of selfishness. What a liberation it is when you can forgive. Here again we see that we are not a wilderness, but a garden of the Lord, when we give our lives to Jesus. He does the job.

# 11

# Lizzy

We had to live in beds stacked one on top of another. There were three beds in each stack, and above the cots where my sister Betsie and I slept, there lived a girl, Lizzy, who was a prostitute. Every day Betsie gathered the people around us, and she or I gave a little Bible talk. Lizzy did not join us, but she always listened, and once I heard Betsie talking with her.

"I do not know if I can come to Jesus," Lizzy said to Betsie.

"Why not? The Lord loves you. You are very precious in God's eyes, and when you come to Jesus, He will not send you away. He has never sent anyone away who came to seek forgiveness and to find the answer for his sin or guilt problem.

"God made this world good, and human beings were without sin, but then we people started to do wrong things, and God had to punish us. But He loved us so much that He had a talk with His Son, Jesus, and God said, 'What must I do? I have to punish people, but I love them.'

"Jesus said, 'Father, I will go to the world, and I will carry their punishment.' And the Father agreed. Jesus came to this world and He lived here for thirty-three years. That must have been a difficult time for Him, even from the beginning, for He was used to being in heaven, and then He came to such a dark world, full of problems.

"The most terrible thing He experienced was when He was crucified. Crucifixion is a very cruel, torturous way to kill people. He could have been saved from that. There were many angels around Him, and had Jesus told them to keep Him from the Cross, they would have done so. But He did not ask them, because He was willing to suffer and die. It was His purpose, when He came into this world, to die for your sins and mine.

"Now when we believe in Him we do not have to fear any punishment. We are free! There will be a Judgment Day and every one of us will be present there, but we have nothing to fear when we believe in the Lord Jesus Christ. There is no condemnation for those who belong to Him. And Jesus Himself is our Judge and Advocate. You can read that in the Bible."

> Who then will condemn us? Will Christ? *No!* For he is the one who died for us and came back to life again for us and is sitting at the place of highest honor next to God, pleading for us there in heaven.
>
> Romans 8:34 LB

"But I don't do what I should do!" said Lizzy.

"I don't believe that you must do anything," replied Betsie. "Believe in the Lord Jesus Christ and you will be saved. What had to be done has all been done by Jesus Christ. Your part is to accept that at the Cross He died for your sins."

Lizzy folded her hands and said, "Thank You, Jesus, that You did it all at the Cross. I surely am not able to do much to change myself, but I thank You that You will do it in me."

# 12

# The Red Ticket

"Fall in for the street commando!"

Making streets was heavy work. Betsie and I showed our red tickets, which we had just received from the *Aufseherin*. They were the sign that we were unable to do hard labor. We climbed on our cot and hummed a little song. We picked up the stockings, which we had to knit for the German soldiers.

"You seem to be happy," said the woman behind us.

"We certainly are. We were called to enroll in the street commando, and look what we have." We showed the red tickets.

The woman smiled cynically. "Do you know what your red tickets mean? At the first cleaning up of prisoners, all the red-ticket owners disappear into the gas chamber."

We stopped humming our song. I looked through the window at the smoke which was going up from the crematorium and I thought, "When will my time come to be killed?"

Betsie saw what I was looking at. "Are you afraid, Corrie?"

Afraid? Of what?
To feel the Spirit's glad release?
To pass from pain to perfect peace?
The strife and strain of life to cease?
Afraid of that?

I knew that my sins were forgiven, that my name was in the Book of Life, and that I had received Jesus as my Saviour. He had made me a child of God. Jesus gives eternal life. That means the life that belongs to eternity, to heaven. And I had that.

I knew that if they killed me I would go to the Father's house with many mansions. I looked death in the eyes. I saw the valley of the shadow of death. But I was not afraid, for I knew that I would not go alone through that valley. Jesus was going to take my hand and help me through.

How good to know that you belong to Jesus! Do you know it? If not, lay your hand in His strong hand. Those who come to Him, He will in no wise cast out.

# 13

# Ask More–He Will Give

It was crowded and filthy and miserable in that room built for two hundred where seven hundred of us lived together. (There were two such rooms.) Although it was a terrible place, yet there were several things for which I was thankful.

One reason for gratitude was that twice a day Betsie or I could gather the prisoners around us for a little Bible message. First I did it only on Sunday, but when I saw that so many people died or were killed from one Sunday to the next, I decided to risk it every day.

Several of my fellow prisoners really came to the Lord and accepted the Lord Jesus as their Saviour. They decided to come every day for the Bible message. Then I gave the talk in the evenings for those prisoners who were assigned to work elsewhere during the day and couldn't at-

tend the daytime meetings in the area where I
had to knit stockings.

When I finished teaching, there would be many
questions, and I realized that many did not know
the simplest truths of the Bible.

I often talked about the fact that when we pray,
the Lord hears our prayers. He loves us and loves
to have us talk to Him. He always listens when
we pray. I told them about the miracles that actu-
ally happened to me when God answered my
prayers. Sometimes He does not answer our
prayers in the way we want or expect Him to
answer. We will understand why one day when
we are in heaven.

I told them the story of a blind man who came
to Jesus during the time that Jesus was in the
world with us. Jesus healed him, and then He
asked the man, "Can you see?"

The man said, "I see men like trees walking."
Jesus touched his eyes again, and the man said,
"Now I can see clearly." (Read this in Mark
8:23–25.)

You know, sometimes when you first come to
Jesus, it is as if you do not see so very much and
you do not understand what is happening. You
are not able to enjoy your new life. Then the best

thing you can do is to tell the Lord that you do not understand it, that you do not see clearly, and that you really see man as the blind man did—like walking trees.

If Jesus had not asked this blind man whether he could see, I am sure that nevertheless the man would have told Him, and said, "Lord, I am glad that I can see a little bit, but I do not see enough." Then Jesus would have healed him.

So it is with you and me. If we do not see as much as we need or want to see, then we must tell it to the Lord. He will heal our eyes so that we see that the love of God is far greater than anything else.

There is an ocean of God's love which we discover when we receive Jesus Christ as our Saviour. He shows it to us through His Holy Spirit. God sees you and me. He knows everything about us, and He loves us so much that He wants to help us and do what we ask.

# 14

# Is a *No* Answer an Answer?

When God gives us the *no* answer, it can be a difficult testing of our faith, but when we study the Bible, we understand more and more that God never makes a mistake. Once we are in heaven, we will understand it all.

My life is like a weaving between my God
   and me,
I do not choose the colors, He worketh stead-
   ily.
Ofttimes He weaveth sorrow and I in foolish
   pride,
Forget He sees the upper, and I the under-
   side.

I once prayed for Betsie, my sister. She was so *very* ill. Even in the filthy bunk in our barrack or at our work, it was such a joy and comfort for us

48

just to be together night and day. Now she was in that primitive hospital, and our friends and I, who loved her so, prayed that the Lord would heal her. But when I returned to the hospital after roll call and looked through the window, I saw that she had died. That was one of the darkest moments of my life.

I could not understand why God had not answered my prayer. A few days later, I was called out of lineup and I heard that I was to be set free. I had to go through the office on my way out, and I learned that they did not know my sister had died. I asked them, "What about my sister?" I wanted to find out what would have happened to her if she had still been alive.

They said, "Your sister must remain here for the duration of the war."

"May I remain with my sister?"

"Not for a minute! Now get out!"

I have praised and thanked my Lord for that unanswered prayer. Just imagine how it would have been if she had been healed, and would have had to stay in the hell of Ravensbruck without me. I would have returned to my homeland tormented night and day by the consciousness of her suffering. I saw God's side of the embroidery.

# 15

# Freedom

It was 3:30 A.M. I woke up, and my first thought was, *Roll call*. I looked around me. Clean windows, a chair, a table, a picture on the wall. I was no longer in prison. I was free!

I could sleep for several more hours but I did not. I got up and started to write down what I had experienced in the three prisons. Those writings became my first book, *A Prisoner and Yet . . . .* It became a best seller in Holland, because people were interested in reading about what had happened to the victims of the concentration camps.

For many years of my life I had been the leader of Girl Guide clubs (European Girl Scouts). As soon as I recovered my strength a bit, I got together with all the girls I could locate to tell them what I had experienced, and to find out what had happened to them.

After much talk together, they asked, "What are you going to do?" We were sitting in a clubhouse, cross-legged on the floor. My club girls were interested in all I had learned in prison—that difficult class in life's school.

"Girls, I'm so thankful that all my tomorrows are in God's hands. I want to tell you what happened one night." And this was what I told them:

It was midnight in Ravensbruck, and Betsie tried to wake me up. Sleep was such an important thing. You forgot that you were in prison.

"Why are you waking me up? Leave me, please, in the world of dreams, where there are no guards, no barbed wire, and no lice."

Betsie put her coat over our heads so that we could talk without disturbing our fellow prisoners. "I have to talk with you, Corrie. God has told me several things which we must do after the war, and I am afraid that I may forget some of His instructions.

"We have learned so much here, and now we must go all over the world to tell people what we now know—that Jesus' light is stronger than the deepest darkness. Only prisoners can know how desperate this life is. We can tell from experience that no pit is too deep, because God's everlasting arms always sustain us.

"We must rent a concentration camp after the war, where we can help displaced Germans to get a roof over their heads. I have heard that 95 percent of the houses in Germany are bombed out. No one will want these concentration camps after the war, so we must rent one and help the German people to find a new life in a destroyed Germany. God has shown me in a vision, a house in Holland in which we will receive the Dutch prisoners who survive the concentration camps. We will help them to find their way through life again."

I asked her, "Must we stay in that camp which we will open for the people here in Germany, or will we be able to stay in the house for the ex-prisoners, at home in Holland?"

"Neither," Betsie said. "You must travel all over the world and tell everybody who will listen what we have learned here—that Jesus is a reality and that He is stronger than all the powers of darkness. Tell them. Tell everyone who will listen! He is our greatest Friend, our hiding place."

A week later Betsie died. A week after that I

was set free, and only one week later, the Germans put to death all the women of my age in Ravensbruck.

I looked at my Girl Guides who had listened to my story. "Girls," I said, "I know that you are sincerely interested in what I am going to do. My answer is that I will obey all the instructions that God gave to me through Betsie."

I obeyed. You can read about many of my adventures over the years in my book *Tramp for the Lord.*

Since I have often visited in prisons, now I want to talk with you about some of these experiences.

# 16

# Kimio

While visiting a prison in Africa, I heard about a young man who was sentenced to die. I asked to see him, but the prison officials would allow me to enter his cell only if three soldiers went in with me.

The cell had a very high ceiling and one small window at the top for light. It was bare, except for a shelf very low to the ground. Sitting on that shelf was a handsome black African who had one more week to live. I was praying very hard! I wanted to be able to talk with him as if we were alone, but the soldiers made me uncomfortable. I always reacted that way when I was around men with guns.

As we talked, I learned that the young man's name was Kimio and that he had a wife and children. Kimio knew about the Cross, and that Jesus had died there for the sins of the whole world, including his sins.

I asked him if he knew who was responsible for his arrest and imprisonment. He was a political prisoner, and there came into his eyes the darkness of hatred.

"I can name every person responsible for my being here," he said.

"Can you forgive them?"

"No, I can't."

"I understand that. Once a man betrayed me and my whole family. Because of his betrayal, four of my family died in prison, and I suffered in three of the most horrible prisons in the whole world.

"And, Kimio, I could forgive that man. Not through my own strength—never—but through the Lord. The Holy Spirit can fill your heart with God's love, and He can give you the power to forgive. Kimio, I felt so free after I had forgiven that man. You have to die very soon."

"Yes, and I have a wife and children that I will never see again because of those men."

"I understand, Kimio, but you have to come before God. You have to face a righteous God very soon, and you know about Jesus at the Cross.

"Jesus said, 'If you do not forgive those who wrong you, my Heavenly Father will not forgive you.' So Kimio, you *have* to forgive.

"You are unable, but the Holy Spirit in you *is* able. Just pray this prayer with me. 'Thank You, Jesus, that You have brought into my heart God's love through the Holy Spirit. Thank You, Father, that Your love in me is stronger than my hatred.' "

I don't remember what else Kimio and I talked about after that, but I no longer felt the presence of those three armed soldiers. There was the presence of angels in that cell. I learned later that Kimio wrote to his wife: "Love the people who have brought me here. Forgive them. You can't, and I can't, but Jesus *in* us is able."

Kimio was trapped by the misery of this world, but he learned how to be free.

# 17

# Joy? Is That Possible?

The worst prison I have ever seen was in another area of Africa. The building was too small for all the prisoners. Only half of them could go inside the building at night; the rest had to stay outside.

During the day they were all kept crammed together in the dirty compound in front of the prison. There had been a tropical rainstorm, and the ground was one large pool of mud. I saw that some men had branches on which they were sitting. Some had small pieces of paper, and others had little shelves. They had all struggled to find something to sit on. Everything was dark and black, but the darkest was the expression of their faces.

I often pray at the same time I am speaking, saying one thing to the Lord and another to the people who are listening to my talk. On this day I said, "Lord, give me a message for these men that will help them in this very difficult place where they live."

The answer from the Lord was, "What is the fruit of the Spirit?" I knew it:

> The fruit of the Spirit is love, joy, peace, long-suffering, gentleness, goodness, faith.
>
> *See* Galatians 5:22 RSV

Then the Lord said, "Speak about joy."

"Lord, how can I speak about joy to these people who live in this terrible place?"

The answer was, "My Holy Spirit is here in this place, and the fruit of the Spirit is available wherever you are."

Then I remembered that when I had been in prison I had found joy even in the midst of the most desperate surroundings. When we are powerless to do a thing, it is a great joy that we can come and step inside the ability of Jesus.

"Lord," I said, "You are able to give joy." Then I heard myself giving a very happy message. The faces of the men lit up when I told them that the joy of the Lord can be our strength, even when we are in very difficult circumstances.

The only thing necessary to begin moving into the joy of the Lord is to tell Jesus Christ that you would like to be His follower. "Receive Jesus Christ as your Saviour and Lord, and He will give you the joy," I said.

Many did. I could see it in their faces. But I also saw faces of people who were not ready or willing. They remained just as dark and unhappy as before.

I said to them, "Fellows, I can understand that you think such joy is not possible for you when you are in this prison, but I can tell you that I was in a prison far worse than yours, where only 20 percent of us came out alive. The rest all starved or were killed in a cruel way. But the Lord Jesus was with us. His Holy Spirit was in our hearts, and there was often a great joy.

"There is joy for you, too, but you must be at peace with God and man—that *is* possible! When you confess your sins to the Lord, He is faithful and just, and He forgives you. He removes your sins, He cleanses your heart, and He fills you with the Holy Spirit. The fruit of the Spirit is joy."

Finally I asked, "Who is willing to receive Jesus Christ? Raise your hand."

All the prisoners did, and even the guards who

were there did, too! Now, when *everyone* raises his hand to accept Jesus Christ, then I do not always trust it, but I looked into their faces and saw that this time it was real for all of them.

When I went to the car to leave for the next place, all the men and the guards accompanied me to the street. They were standing around the car, shouting something which I could not understand. I asked the missionary who was with me, "What are these men saying?"

She smiled and said, "They are all shouting, 'Come again, old woman. Come again and tell us more about Jesus.'"

I was so glad! You know, I had to leave, but the Lord stayed with these men, and the Holy Spirit filled their hearts. It is true that when you lay your weak hand in the strong hand of Jesus, He keeps you from falling and never leaves you alone.

# 18

# Three Decent Sinners

The Apostle Paul was in prison. It must have been terrible for him. His hands were chained to the hands of two guards night and day. He never knew from one day to the next what the enemy was intending to do with him.

We do know some of the things that Paul did while a prisoner. He wrote letters, which you should read. Some of these "epistles" you should read are called Ephesians, Philippians, Colossians, and the two letters to Timothy.

Another thing we know about Paul is that he used his time in prison to bring the Gospel to the people around him. These men to whom he was chained could not run away when he preached. And what was the result? People were converted! At the very end of his letter to the Philippian Church, Paul writes:

> Greetings to every true Christian, from me and
> all the brothers here with me. All the Christians
> here would like to send their best wishes, par-
> ticularly those who belong to the Emperor's
> household.
>
> Philippians 4:21, 22 PHILLIPS

I once spoke about this in a prison in New Zealand, because I believe that every prisoner can
help his fellow prisoners to know and receive
Jesus Christ. Prisoners can be reached by their
fellow prisoners better than by people from outside, because they understand one another.

I know some of you are thinking what some of
the prisoners there in New Zealand thought:
"Perhaps God can use other people, but not me. I
am not good enough."

Do you know what happened there? One of the
prisoners suddenly stood up and said, "Fellows,
this morning I read in the Bible about three murderers. One's name was Paul, one was Moses, and
the other was David. We know them as heroes of
God, but all three were murderers. What God can
do with a totally surrendered murderer! There is
hope for you and me, fellows!"

Yes, there is hope for you who read this. I believe I have never heard such a good sermon as that one from a man who was a prisoner. What God can do with you when you surrender all is *tremendous!* There is one condition:

Stay always within the boundaries where God's love can reach and bless you.

Jude 21 LB

I have a glove. This glove cannot do anything, but when my hand is in the glove, the glove can do many things. It can drive a car, it can write.

Yes, I know, it is not the glove that does it, it is the hand inside the glove. You and I are—and Moses, David, and Paul were—just gloves. It was the Holy Spirit in them, and in you and me, who does the work.

What we have to do is to make room for the Holy Spirit, and then miracles can happen in our lives. Perhaps you think, "Oh, that is possible for a *mature* Christian, for somebody who knows the Bible well, and has had training." Perhaps you even think you must first go to a Bible school. All these things are good, but the Lord can also use you when you have none of these opportunities.

# 19

# Hi, Brother!

Let me tell you about a prisoner I met some years ago in Bermuda. I had spoken to a big group in the prison, and a black guard asked me, "Will you go with me to some cells where there are people who really need your advice?" I went into that part of the prison where the men were kept who were not even allowed to attend the meetings.

I saw two men in a cell. One of them had a round, red rag on his back.

"Has that man tried to run away?" I asked the guard.

"Yes," he replied. "How do you know that?"

"Because of the red rag on the back of his uniform. I have been in three prisons, and we were also forced to wear red rags on our uniforms, if we tried to run away."

"This man is a murderer, and he was sentenced to whippings. He was so afraid of the whippings that he tried to run away. Poor fellow, he has had a double portion."

When I saw him sitting there on the floor, the expression on his face reminded me of a wounded animal, and my heart went out to him. I prayed, "Lord, help me to find a way to his heart." I went to him with my Bible in my hand and asked him, "Say, fellow, have you had a whipping?"

"Yes."

"Was it bad?"

"Yes."

"Did they take you to the hospital afterwards?"

"No, it was not that serious."

He stood up and came to the barred door, probably thinking to himself, "That woman is sure asking me strange questions!"

Then I asked, "Did they treat your wounds?"

"Yes, they did. They rubbed them."

"Is there hatred in your heart?"

"Hatred? My whole heart and my whole life are full of hatred."

"I can understand that."

"*Ha! You?*"

Then I told him how I had felt when they whipped my sister, because she was too frail and weak to shovel sand. How hatred had come into my heart!

But I said, "Fellow, a miracle happened then. Jesus brought into my heart God's love through the Holy Spirit, and I had no hatred. I could forgive.

"And when you receive Jesus Christ as your Saviour, He will fill your heart—not with hatred but with love. How do you do it? You just come to Him and say, 'Lord Jesus, will You be my Saviour?' The Lord is willing to be that. Then you must ask Him to come into your heart. And He *will* come, because it is written in the Bible, and the Bible is true. Jesus said:

> Behold, I stand at the door, and knock: if any man hear my voice, and open the door, I will come in to him . . . .
>
> Revelation 3:20

"Fellow, when the Lord Jesus comes into your heart, there is love in your heart. The worst may happen in your life, but the best remains."

I prayed with that man, and then he prayed. I believe I had never heard such a strange prayer.

The man had never prayed before, but one of the things he did was thank Jesus that He had died for him on the Cross.

Have you ever thanked Jesus for that?

I shook hands with the man. Then he said, "Have you another five minutes?"

"Sure. Why?"

"On the other side of the corridor, in the third cell, is a man in great darkness. Please, tell him also of Jesus."

I went to the man in the third cell. I told him about Jesus, and how I prayed for him! When you speak about Jesus, you can always pray at the same time. You can have the vertical and the horizontal connection at the same moment.

The man in the third cell said his *yes* to Jesus. I mean a real *yes*—a decision.

I had to leave the prison then, but I first passed the cell of the murderer. "Say, fellow, that was good that you sent me to the third cell. He also has accepted Jesus Christ as his Saviour and Lord."

The man looked around me and shouted across the corridor, "Hi, brother!" A babe in Christ, a few minutes old, and he already had a burden for souls. How old are you?

When someone becomes a Christian he becomes a brand new person inside. He is not the same any more. A new life has begun! All these new things are from God who brought us back to himself through what Christ Jesus did. And God has given us the privilege of urging everyone to come into his favor and be reconciled to him. For God was in Christ, restoring the world to himself, no longer counting men's sins against them but blotting them out. This is the wonderful message he has given us to tell others. We are Christ's ambassadors. God is using us to speak to you: we beg you, as though Christ himself were here pleading with you, receive the love he offers you—be reconciled to God.

2 Corinthians 5:17–20 LB

# 20

# Corrie's Message

In New Zealand I visited a small prison, where there were probably no more than fourteen men. We had a good time together. The men were sitting with their backs against a wall, and I was sitting in front of them, speaking about the great joy of knowing that you are a child of God.

I told them that when you ask Jesus to come into your heart and you confess your sins, then He does a great miracle in your heart, which He Himself calls "being born into the family of God." At that time you may say to God, "Father, my Father." And He says to you, "My child."

Four of these men made a decision. Each wanted to give his heart to Jesus, to be cleansed and born into the Kingdom of God—to be born a child of God.

Before I left, I shook hands with all the men.

One was a very old man. He cried and held my
hand and kissed it. I was a little bit amused about
that, and finally said, "Now, friend, let me go,
and the Lord bless you." Then he let go of my
hand.

This man was sentenced to a long imprisonment for the crime of manslaughter. The woman
with whom he lived had snored one night when
he was drunk. He strangled her because of her
noise. When he realized that the woman was
dead, he was so scared he ran straight to the
police and told them, "I have murdered my
wife."

"Why are you crying so?" I asked him.

He replied, "Because I am so happy. I have
always had such terrible feelings of guilt because
I killed the woman I lived with. Now I have
brought it to the Lord Jesus, and I know I am
forgiven. I am a child of God! Jesus is in my
heart."

A year later I went back to that prison, and I
talked with some of the men there. I asked where
the old man was, and they told me, "He died
some time ago."

One of the men took me aside and said, "I must

tell you something. Whenever that man heard me going through the corridor, he called me into his cell. He would say, 'Let us talk about Corrie's message.' "

How happy I was that the Lord had used me to help that man!

# 21

# Conversations in Prisons

I know there are almost insurmountable problems when you are in prison. I would like to write about some of the problems we discussed when I talked with prisoners in America.

### Ann

"What is the most difficult thing that you have to go through?" I asked Ann.

I sat with her in her cell in solitary confinement. She showed me a photograph of her husband and children. "Because of my crime, I have given them such a hard life. They lack a wife and mother and they have to bear the shame—all because of the bad things I have done."

She told me that she had accepted Jesus as her

Saviour ten years ago, but had solidly backslid. She knew much about the Bible, so it was easy to talk with her.

"There is an answer to your problem, Ann. It is Jesus. He has told us that we may pray for one another. You can pray for your children and your husband. You can tell the Lord everything. He understands you better than any human being.

"I read in the Book of Revelation that not one of our prayers is lost. They are kept in heaven. That is how important they are in our Heavenly Father's eyes.

"You feel guilty that your family has to suffer because of you. You carry that guilt. I have a book here. It must lie somewhere: on my hand, on the table, or on the floor. It is the same with your guilt. It must lie somewhere. It is lying on you. You are carrying it.

"Now the Bible teaches us a mystery. When Jesus died on the Cross, God laid on Him the guilt of the whole world. Jesus was willing to bear that terrible death, to carry our sins, our guilt. You may bring your sins, your guilt to Jesus, and He will forgive you and make you clean. Then He will fill you with the Holy Spirit. The fruit of the Spirit is peace and joy and love. Then you will be able to think of your husband and children with peace."

Ann said, "I believe all you tell me, but I cannot accept it now. I have been away from the Lord for so long. Ten years ago I could have accepted it, but now it is too late."

"Ann, do you remember the story of the lost sheep? A shepherd had one hundred sheep. One evening when he came home, he saw that one sheep was lost. What did he do?

"He left the ninety-nine at home and went to look for that one lost sheep. He found it, took it on his shoulder, and brought it home.

"You are a lost sheep. Jesus will bring you home. The shepherd rejoiced and organized a feast to celebrate the finding of the lost sheep. Jesus rejoices when He finds you. Only tell Him everything. He loves you. Confess your sins to Him and ask Him to come into your heart. He will rejoice, and you will rejoice."

Ann did it. And I know Jesus rejoiced!

### Frank

"Trust and study the Bible, Frank. It is the Word of God. You have asked Jesus to come into your life, and He came. Now all the promises of the Bible are yours."

Frank had seen one of Billy Graham's meetings on television and he had joined the many who came to Jesus that evening.

"Do you know what my problem is when I read the Bible?" Frank said. "It all happened so very long ago. I have seen Christians who were really happy, but after a while they backslid. Their Christianity did not last long."

"Frank, what can help you and give you solid ground to stand on is your faith in Jesus. He is the same yesterday, today, and tomorrow. He never changes. He is the same now as He was in Israel two thousand years ago. He is a solid rock to stand upon.

On Christ the solid rock, I stand.
All other ground is sinking sand.

"Talk much with Him. He is here *now*. He loves and understands you."

## Roger

He was a young man in a big prison. I had spoken in the chapel, and while he cleaned the table where we had had some refreshments, I had an opportunity to talk with him.

Without looking up, he said, "I am afraid."

"Who are you afraid of? The guards?"

"No, the men around me. They say that they will kill me if I do not do what they ask me to do. They tell me to do dirty things, which I cannot refuse."

"Roger, I was in a prison where the devil was strong, and I was afraid, like you are. I saw then that I was weak, and the devil was stronger, much stronger than I. But then I saw Jesus, who is much stronger than the devil. Jesus and I together could overcome the devil. When I realized that, miracles happened.

"Paul, in the Bible, had a problem in his life. The Bible does not tell us exactly what it was, but he calls it a 'thorn in the flesh, messenger of Satan, to harass me.'

"You can read about it in Second Corinthians 12:7–10. Paul asked God to take it away, but God did not remove that thing. He answered Paul, 'My grace is sufficient for you, for my power is made perfect in weakness.' God does not always remove difficult things from our lives, but His grace in us *is* sufficient to overcome the difficulties."

Have you got any rivers you think are uncrossable?
Got any mountains you can't tunnel through?
God specializes in things called impossible.
He can do what no other can do.

# 22

# Mike

"I am going on parole next week."

"Boy, that is good! Are you glad?"

"No, this was my fourth time in prison, and soon it will be my fifth. I know myself."

"No, Mike, Jesus has found you, you have found Jesus, and you and He together will overcome the temptations. Read the story of Gideon in Judges 6.

"Gideon was neither strong nor courageous. He hid himself in a barn, in the bottom of a winepress. But how did God see him? The angel who came to him said, 'The Lord is with you, you mighty man of valor.' Because the Lord was with Him, Gideon changed from a weakling into a strong overcomer. The Lord said to him, 'Go in this your strength.'

"Mike, the devil is stronger—much stronger

than you and me—but Jesus is much stronger than the devil, and with Jesus, we are stronger than the devil.

"It is important that you do what Jude said, 'Stay always within the boundaries where God's love can reach and bless you' (Jude 21 LB).

"If, when you leave prison, you go straight to a bar and get yourself drunk and renew your relationship with the friends who helped you to go to prison through their advice and assistance in your crimes, you can be sure that you will find yourself in this building for the fifth time. You stand on victory ground with Jesus, but you must be willing to go the whole way with Him. You are free to choose."

"That is exactly my problem. I am willing now to be a good guy, but what happens when I am free?"

"Mike, you are not the only one who has this problem, but the Lord knows that. The Bible supplies the answer when it says, 'Be filled with the Spirit' in Ephesians 5:18. A Spirit-filled Christian is a difficult target for the enemy, for he has the fruit of the Spirit and the gifts of the Holy Spirit, which are like a good armor and weapons in his hand. A compromise with the enemy is deadly dangerous, just as if a soldier on the front line helps the enemy to attack him and his fellow soldiers.

"If, again and again, you lay your weak hand in the strong hand of Jesus, you will be able to remain within the boundaries where God's love can reach and bless you."

"How do you do that? It all sounds so nice when you say it, but how do I lay my hand in Jesus' hand?"

"Get used to telling Jesus everything. He understands you and loves you. You might say to Him, 'Jesus, I need money badly. I can make a lot of money quickly if I go to that bar and plan a little job with one of my friends. I can also get something to drink there, and I really want a drink. Jesus. Take my hand, fill me with Your Holy Spirit. Keep me from falling!'

"If you say that, Jesus will help you. He is not only willing, but also able to help you. Ask Him to help you find people who love Him and who are willing to show you how to understand the Bible. Fellowship is so important. Read the Bible much. When you find a text that helps you more than others, write it down, and put it in your pocket, and learn it by heart.

"Mike, the most important thing is *trust Jesus.* He will help your faith to grow. In Hebrews 12 He is called the author and finisher of your faith. I like helping you very much, and pray that the Lord will give me wisdom on advising you. Jesus likes to help you even more, and He *really* is able to help."

# 23

# Joe

"I heard your talk today about how to become a child of God by Jesus Christ. It made me anxious to do it. But, lady, you do not know what kind of a guy I am. I have murdered people, and don't ask me how! Let's be honest—I am a lousy guy. No, I am not made of the wood from which you can cut and shape a Christian."

"Joe, there are two ways that we know our sins. The devil accuses us night and day. I don't know if you know the devil. I know him. He speaks very clearly, and he says, 'What you have done is what you are, and what you will always be. There is no hope for you.'

"The devil is a liar! The Bible tells us something different. When you bring your sins to Jesus, when you confess your sins, He is faithful and just to forgive you, and He will cleanse you with His blood. You don't understand that? It does not matter. He does it, and it works!

"The Bible also promises that He will put your sins as far away from you as the east is from the west. It is as though He has cast them into the depths of the sea—forgiven and forgotten."

I met Joe again a month later. He looked quite different. The first thing he said was, "I have done it! I was totally miserable! They put me in the hole, which I had feared they would do. I had been in there before for a very long time.

"On my first day in it again, I figured I had nothing to lose and I said, 'God, if You do exist, take this miserable life of mine in Your hand.' At that very moment something happened. It was as if I was no longer alone. I can't tell you exactly how it was, but I felt happier than ever before. Was it the Lord who came to me? I could suddenly talk to Him. I remembered everything you had said and I asked myself, 'Is what she said true?'

"I slept better that night than I had for weeks, and when I woke up, I felt that happy feeling again. I must say that the weeks I spent in the hole were happy. I knew I was not alone, and to my amazement, I was taken out of the hole after only two weeks.

"Now, Miss ten Boom, I believe it all! How good it is to read the Bible. You had told me that Jesus knocks at the door of your heart, and so I said, 'Come in.' I have told Him more than anyone else all that I have done wrong and through that, I believe there was a clearing up of the dirty mess."

"Joe, you can read in John 3 what took place in your life. In that chapter Jesus tells about what happens when you accept Him. You were born again. Now God is your Father, Joe, and what a Friend you have in Jesus! I'm so glad that the Bible is not fantasy. It is not imagination, not feelings, not philosophy—it is reality! The greatest reality is that Jesus is here on this earth right now, through His Holy Spirit. You are here. I am here. Jesus is here, too."

# 24

# So Long!

When you believe the Lord Jesus Christ and you ask Him to come into your heart and into your life, He gives you *His* freedom and a new dimension of living that circumstances cannot destroy.

We can all get to heaven
Without health—
Without wealth—
Without fame—
Without learning—
Without culture—
Without beauty—
Without friends—
Without ten thousands of things.
But we can never get to heaven without Christ.

God promises us forgiveness for what we have done, but we need His deliverance from what we *are*. He conquered death at the Cross and He went to heaven. He pleads for us there.

At the same time He is in heaven, He is also with us! I do not understand it at all, but I know it works. I have experienced His presence in the deepest hell that man can create. I have really tested the promises of the Bible, and believe me, you can count on them.

I know that Jesus Christ can live in us—in you and me—through His Holy Spirit. We can talk with Him. We can tell Him everything. You can talk with Him out loud or in your heart—when you are alone, as I was alone in solitary confinement, or in a place crowded with people. The joy is that He hears each word!

In Ravensbruck, after a terrible winter, it was decided that all prisoners my age and older should be killed. One week before this was to happen, I was set free. Later, I learned that it was done only because of a clerical error. In rerecording our numbers, my number had mistakenly been transferred from the death column to freedom!

A blunder of man, yes. But I knew it was God's

way of telling me that I must share—for the rest of my life—what I had learned about Him.

That is why I wanted to write this book for you. I am eighty-five years old now, and I know that the moment is coming when I will have to die. But I am not afraid of death. I belong to Jesus. All of my tomorrows are in His hands.

You know, eternal life does not start when you go to heaven. It starts the moment you reach out to Jesus. That is where it *all* begins. He never turned His back on anyone, and He is waiting for *you!* God bless you.

# Appendix of Helpful Scriptures

The Bible is a source of strength and wisdom. Read the Word of God often. I have written down some texts which have helped me. I pray that the Lord will bless these texts and this book for *you*.

### Feeling Alone

Be strong and of good courage, do not fear or be in dread of them: for it is the Lord your God who goes with you; he will not fail you or forsake you.

Deuteronomy 31:6 RSV

It is the Lord who goes before you; he will be with you, he will not fail you or forsake you; do not fear or be dismayed.

Deuteronomy 31:8 RSV

"Come to me, all who labor and are heavy laden,

and I will give you rest. Take my yoke upon you, and learn from me; for I am gentle and lowly in heart, and you will find rest for your souls. For my yoke is easy, and my burden is light."

Matthew 11:28–30 RSV

". . . I give them eternal life, and they shall never perish, and no one shall snatch them out of my hand. My Father, who has given them to me, is greater than all, and no one is able to snatch them out of the Father's hand."

John 10:28, 29 RSV

"If a man loves me, he will keep my word, and my Father will love him, and we will come to him and make our home with him."

John 14:23 RSV

[Jesus said,] ". . . I will never fail you nor forsake you." Hence we can confidently say,

> "The Lord is my helper,
> I will not be afraid;
> what can man do to me?"

Hebrews 13:5, 6 RSV

## Temptation

No temptation has overtaken you that is not common to man. God is faithful, and he will not let you be tempted beyond your strength, but with the temptation will also provide the way of escape, that you may be able to endure it.

1 Corinthians 10:13 RSV

Do you want more and more of God's kindness and peace? Then learn to know him better and better. For as you know him better, he will give you, through his great power, everything you need for living a truly good life: he even shares his own glory and his own goodness with us! And by that same mighty power he has given us all the other rich and wonderful blessings he promised; for instance, the promise to save us from the lust and rottenness all around us, and to give us his own character . . . . Then you must learn to know God better and discover what he wants you to do. Next, learn to put aside your own desires so that you will become patient and godly, gladly letting God have his way with you. This will make possible the next step, which is for you to enjoy other people and to like them, and finally you will grow to love them deeply. The more you

go on in this way, the more you will grow strong
spiritually and become fruitful and useful to our
Lord Jesus Christ.

2 Peter 1:2–8 LB

Stay always within the boundaries where God's
love can reach and bless you. Wait patiently for
the eternal life that our Lord Jesus Christ in his
mercy is going to give you. Try to help those who
argue against you. Be merciful to those who
doubt. Save some by snatching them as from the
very flames of hell itself. And as for others, help
them to find the Lord by being kind to them, but
be careful that you yourselves aren't pulled along
into their sins. Hate every trace of their sin while
being merciful to them as sinners.

Jude 21–23 LB

How can a young man stay pure? By reading your
Word and following its rules . . . . I have
thought much about your words, and stored them
in my heart so that they would hold me back from
sin.

Psalms 119:9, 11 LB

**Worry**

"Therefore I tell you, do not be anxious about your life, what you shall eat or what you shall drink, nor about your body, what you shall put on. Is not life more than food, and the body more than clothing? Look at the birds of the air; they neither sow nor reap nor gather into barns, and yet your heavenly Father feeds them. Are you not of more value than they? And which of you by being anxious can add one cubit to his span of life? And why are you anxious about clothing? Consider the lilies of the field, how they grow; they neither toil nor spin; yet I tell you, even Solomon in all his glory was not arrayed like one of these. But if God so clothes the grass of the field, which today is alive and tomorrow is thrown into the oven, will he not much more clothe you, O men of little faith? Therefore do not be anxious, saying, 'What shall we eat?' or 'What shall we drink?' or 'What shall we wear?' For the Gentiles seek all these things; and your heavenly Father knows that you need them all. But seek first his kingdom and his righteousness, and all these things shall be yours as well."

Matthew 6:25–34 RSV